DEC 14

CRETE PUBLIC LIBRARY DISTRICT

S0-BMX-303

An Insider's Guide to

VOLLEYBALL

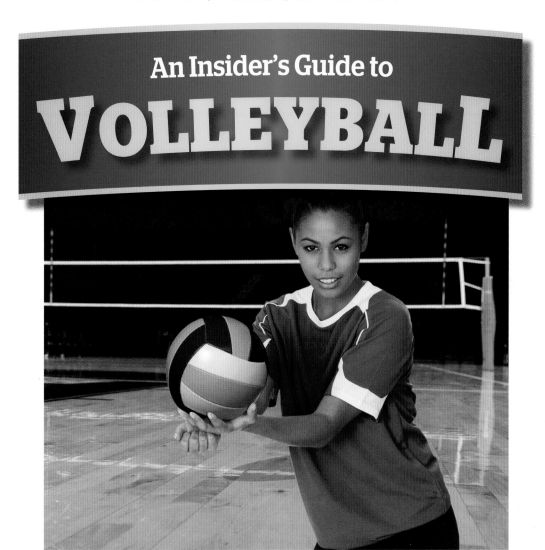

ABIGAEL MCINTYRE, SANDRA GIDDENS, AND OWEN GIDDENS

rosen publishing's
rosen central®

NEW YORK

CRETE PUBLIC LIBRARY
1177 N. MAIN
CRETE, IL 60417
703/672-8017

Published in 2015 by The Rosen Publishing Group, Inc.
29 East 21st Street, New York, NY 10010

Copyright © 2015 by The Rosen Publishing Group, Inc.

First Edition

All rights reserved. No part of this book may be reproduced in any form without permission in writing from the publisher, except by a reviewer.

Library of Congress Cataloging-in-Publication Data

McIntyre, Abigael.
An insider's guide to volleyball/Abigael McIntyre, Sandra Giddens, and Owen Giddens.
    pages cm.—(Sports tips, techniques, and strategies)
Includes bibliographical references and index.
ISBN 978-1-4777-8595-9 (library bound)—ISBN 978-1-4777-8596-6 (pbk.)—
ISBN 978-1-4777-8598-0 (6-pack)
1. Volleyball—Juvenile literature. 2. Volleyball—Training—Juvenile literature. I. Title.
GV1015.34.M35 2015
796.325—dc23

2013043294

Manufactured in Malaysia

Metric Conversion Chart			
1 inch	2.54 centimeters 25.4 millimeters	1 cup	250 milliliters
1 foot	30.48 centimeters	1 ounce	28 grams
1 yard	.914 meters	1 fluid ounce	30 milliliters
1 square foot	.093 square meters	1 teaspoon	5 milliliters
1 square mile	2.59 square kilometers	1 tablespoon	15 milliliters
1 ton	.907 metric tons	1 quart	.946 liters
1 pound	454 grams	355 degrees F	180 degrees C
1 mile	1.609 kilometers		

6.325
MCI

Contents

CHAPTER 1

Volleyball: A History

Many people have heard of or played the game of volleyball. Did you know that it originated in the United States? The founder of the game was a man by the name of William G. Morgan. He was born in 1870, in a town called Lockport in upstate New York. In 1895, he became the director of physical education for the Young Men's Christian Association (YMCA), in Holyoke, Massachusetts. The YMCA had been founded in London, England, in 1844. It was created by businessmen who saw young men going overboard with unhealthy habits and wanted them to live more productive lives. At the YMCA, basketball was the most popular game at the time, but Morgan, who was in charge of designing physical programs for all ages, felt that he needed another game for the more mature players. He soon invented a game that he named mintonette. The name of the game would later be changed to volleyball.

William G. Morgan is said to be the inventor of volleyball, which was originally known as mintonette.

Morgan felt that basketball, invented in 1891 by his friend James A. Naismith, was just too exhausting for older players. From the game of tennis, he discarded the rackets and raised the height of the net. Then, he asked the Spalding

Manufacturing Company to create a lighter, more responsive version of the basketball. He organized the first volleyball exhibition game in 1896, between local firefighters and city employees at Springfield College. The game was first described in the July 1896 issue of the magazine *Physical Education.*

The game was a combination of basketball, baseball, handball, and tennis. The net was six feet, six inches high, and a varying number of players were on either side of the net. There were not many rules at first, and the ball could be hit many times before it sailed over the net again. The game was nine innings long, like baseball. Each team served three times during each inning. The objective of the game was to keep the ball in play over the net. If the ball hit the net, it was considered a foul. Today, the objective of the game is to make sure that the ball hits the ground within bounds, so the opposing team cannot return it.

In early versions of the game, the ball could be hit any number of times on one side of the net before it was passed to the other.

The YMCA's global reach was responsible for rapidly spreading the interest in volleyball throughout the United States as well as the rest of the world. In 1905, the game was introduced in Cuba. In 1908, it was introduced in Tokyo, and in 1910, China and the Philippines were exposed to this new sport. Filipino players soon developed a new technique in which they hit the ball very high so that another person on their team could position himself to smack the ball down hard on the other side. The set and spike were born! The Filipinos called this technique the *bomba*, which meant the "kill." The player who made the *bomba* was called the *bomberino.*

The popularity of the sport quickly spread to countries all over the world. Pictured above are Japanese women enjoying a game of volleyball.

Volleyball became an integral part of army training. Here, the U.S. Marines play against the Afghan National Army soldiers at ANA Post Nabi.

Volleyball's popularity soon spread to the American army. In fact, during World War I (1914–1917), volleyball became a part of the official training program at military camps around the world. In 1916, volleyball was added to many school and college physical education programs. The first YMCA-sponsored volleyball championships were held in Brooklyn, New York, in 1922 with twenty-seven participating teams from eleven states. In 1928, the United States Volleyball Association was formed. The first Volleyball World Championships were held in 1949 in Prague, Czechoslovakia. In 1957, the International Olympic Committee designated volleyball as an Olympic team sport, and the first Olympic competition was held at the Tokyo games in 1964. Today, there are more than 200 national federations in the Fédération Internationale de Volleyball (FIVB), based in Paris, and an estimated 800 million people play this fun sport at least once a week.

In 1942, William G. Morgan died, never knowing that the game he had created would one day be so popular throughout the world that it would become a thrilling Olympic sport. The Morgan Trophy was established in 1995, 100 years after the game was established, to honor the best female and male college volleyball players in the United States.

Volleyball: Over 100 Years

1895 The game of "mintonette" is created by William G. Morgan, later renamed volleyball in 1897.

1896 The first volleyball team formed at a YMCA in Holyoke, Massachusetts.

1900 Canada is the first foreign country to adopt the game of volleyball.

1905 Volleyball comes to Cuba.

1908 Volleyball spreads to Japan.

1910 Volleyball arrives in China and the Philippines.

1914 Armed forces start playing volleyball.

1916 Filipino players develop the spike.

1928 The U.S. Volleyball Association is founded.

1930 The first two-man beach volleyball game is played in California.

1947 Egypt is the first Arab and African country to organize volleyball activities.

1948 First European Championship held in Rome; Czechoslovakia wins.

1949 The first men's Volleyball World Championship is played.

1964 The first Olympic volleyball tournaments are played in Tokyo; the men's gold medal goes to the USSR and the women's gold goes to Japan.

Israel plays against the U.S.S.R. at the 1952 Men's World Championships.

1973 The first women's World Cup is played in Uruguay; the USSR wins.

1983 The Association of Volleyball Professionals (AVP) is formed.

1984 The United States wins the men's Olympic gold in Los Angeles.

1987 First Beach Volleyball World Championship is played in Ipanema, Brazil.

1988 The U.S. men's team wins its second Olympic gold medal in Seoul, South Korea.

1995 Volleyball is 100 years old; Morgan Trophy is created.

1996 The first Olympic Beach Volleyball Games are held in Atlanta, Georgia. The men's gold goes to the United States. The women's gold goes to Brazil.

2004 Beach Volleyball is played in the evening with artificial lighting for the first time at the Olympics held in Athens, Greece.

Jukka Savio, from Finland, spikes the ball hard to score a point in the European Cup Game in 1979.

The Italian team poses for a photograph during the 1979 Volleyball championship.

CHAPTER 2

The Game

Volleyball, like most other sports, is not limited to a stadium. It can be played in schools, recreation centers, playgrounds, and even on the beach. It can be played at any time of the year, both day and night (of course with lights). Boys and girls of all ages enjoy playing the sport. There are men and women over the age of sixty-five who still actively play volleyball. All you really need for an informal game is a net, a ball, a court, and players. Most players wear lightweight clothes like T-shirts and shorts. In beach volleyball, women sometimes wear two-piece outfits, almost like bikinis.

Jeremy Casebeer and Ryan Doherty compete in the Jose Cuervo Pro Beach Volleyball tournament at Hermosa Beach, California, in 2012.

Beach volleyball evolved from the popular social games of volleyball played on many beaches around the world. It is played on sand courts that can be formed either naturally or built specifically for this purpose. Each team in beach volleyball consists of two players. It is one of the few sports where, on an average, female competitors earn more than males.

In the indoor game, each side consists of six players. The dimensions of the regulation rectangular court are 29.6 feet wide and 59 feet long.

The net, which is over 7 feet high, divides the court into two halves across its width. The net is 32.8 feet long and 3.3 feet wide and is made of black or dark brown mesh string. Poles holding the net are equipped with antennae that extend beyond the height of the net, creating a foul-line marker. The court is also divided by lines. The centerline is directly under the net. There are also lines on each side of the court, parallel to and 10 feet away from the net. These lines are the attack lines. The sidelines and the endlines demarcate the boundary. The server must stand behind the endline when serving the ball.

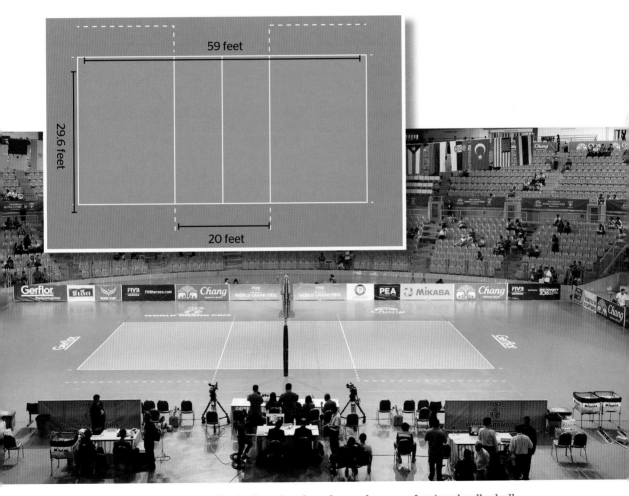

Even though amateur volleyball can be played anywhere, professional volleyball requires a regulation-size court. This court measures 29.6 feet by 59 feet.

When inflated, the volleyball's circumference (the distance around it) is approximately 26 inches, and it weighs around 9 or 10 ounces. It is smaller than a basketball and much bigger than a baseball. The officials in competitive volleyball include a referee, a scorer, an umpire, and line judges.

Volleyball is a game of nonstop motion. The ball is continuously in play. Players can tap the ball, pass it, or hit it. By hitting the ball back and forth over the net with the hands, forearms, head, or any part of the body, play is continued until one team fails to keep the ball in the air or until a rule violation is committed. Catching the ball or hitting it twice in a row is not allowed.

In a match between Italy and Russia, a Russian player
(*in red*) has just served and all other players are waiting in position for the ball.

In addition to the block, the team is allowed to hit the ball three times before returning it to the opposing team. At all times, a team tries to prevent the ball from hitting the ground in their area. In a six-person volleyball team, three players stand near the front of the net, in front of the attack line, and the other three are back-row players or defenders. Any player can pass or set up the ball, but only those in the front row can block or spike the ball. The server stands behind the endline when he or she serves the ball over the net. The ball is tossed into the air and the server strikes it with an open hand or fist. Only one attempt is allowed on the serve. The server keeps serving as long as his or her team continues to win points. Points are scored by successfully landing the ball in the opponents' court without it being returned. The serve must rotate to a new player on the team each time the team wins back the serve.

The player is attempting an overhand serve.

According to the original rules of the game, only the serving team could score points in a volleyball game. This means that if the ball hits the ground on the opposing team's side, play stops and the serving team scores the point. This is called a side-out. The server can serve again. But if the ball hits the ground on the serving side, the play is stopped and the opposing team serves. No point is awarded, because only the serving team can score the point. Before the ball is served, the team rotates, moving clockwise one position, and the person in the back right position becomes the new server. When a hitter on the serving team hits the ball out of bounds, the receiving team does not get the point but gets the chance to serve. If the ball is touched by a member of the receiving team before it goes out of bounds, the point is awarded to the serving team.

The side-out scoring rule was changed in the late 1990s to increase the attraction of the game. In rally scoring, a point is scored on each serve. Rally scoring is used in the deciding game of a match and in international volleyball competitions. Beach volleyball is usually one game, using side-out scoring, or best out of three using rally scoring. In a traditional game, the first team to score 15 points wins. In rally scoring it is 25 points. Usually, a game is over when one team scores 15 points, but the winning team has to succeed by a two-point spread. So a 15 to 14 game, for example, would continue until it became a two-point spread of 16 to 14. A match is a series of games, and to win a match a team must win two out of three or three out of five games.

Just imagine following the ball from your team's side: The server would take hold of it, go behind the endline, and toss it up in the air, striking it so it rises above the net to the opposing team. If it is out of bounds, then the opposing team has to serve it back. If the ball hits the ground on the opposing side, a point is scored for your team. If an opposing player touches the ball, then the players will try to pass the ball toward the net and smack it down on the opposite side. If they manage this, they get to serve and can start winning points.

Players of the U.S. Armed Forces Women's Volleyball team *(in blue)* block an Italian player *(in white)* from scoring during the 3rd Military World Games held in Catania, Sicily, in 2003.

Rules for Indoor Volleyball

Players

- Only six players from each team can play on the court at one time.
- Players cannot touch the net.
- Players cannot cross the centerline.
- The ball is still in play if it touches any part of the sideline or endline.

Service

- A rally begins with a serve from a player behind the endline. The serve must go over the net but can touch the net as long as it goes into the opponent's court.
- On the serve, if the ball does not go over the net or goes out of bounds, the service is lost.
- No second service attempt is permitted.

Ball Contact

- A team is allowed to make contact with the ball three times before clearing the ball over the net.
- A player cannot make contact with the ball with two consecutive touches.
- If a player blocks the ball and the ball continues into his or her court, the team is allowed three touches. A block at the net does not count as a touch.

Actions that End a Rally

- A team touches the ball more than three times before clearing the ball over the net.
    - The ball does not go over the net.
    - The ball hits the ground.
    - The ball hits the ceiling or any object above the court.
    - The ball goes out of bounds.

These players are practicing a rally.

15

How the Game Is Played

The game begins with the service. The underhand serve and the overhand serve are the two most common types of serves. In the underhand serve, the ball is held in one hand, and the other hand swings and hits below and behind the ball. In the overhead serve, the ball is tossed into the air a little bit in front of the server's head. The other hand is pulled back and swung forward to hit the volleyball. Servers start the volley and get one attempt to hit the ball over the net. It is essential to have accurate serves.

The player needs to be alert and agile to save the ball.

This player readies herself for an overhead serve.

The server can also have many styles of serving, just like pitching in baseball. The server can hit a ball with topspin, or serve a fast ball, or serve a deceptive floater that seems to wobble and slip uncertainly in the air.

It is very important for a team to work together to set up passes so that the last person to touch the ball makes a strong and accurate hit at the opposing team. A bump pass or forearm pass is when your arms are extended out straight with your hands locked with thumbs together. The portion of the arm between the elbow and the wrist should hit the ball. The bump pass is used if the team is receiving a serve or if the opposing team has hit the ball with power.

When the knees are bent and the arms are extended over the head, it is called an overhead pass. The fingers are extended after releasing the ball.

A set is the process of moving the ball from player to player until it is positioned properly for the final hitter to hit it over the net effectively. The player passes the ball to his or her teammate, who sets or guides the ball to the hitter. The hitter, of course, tries to win the point by smacking the ball over the net. The setter needs to be able to anticipate the movements of his or her teammates. He or she also needs to recognize the strengths and weaknesses of the opposing team, in order to place the ball where the final hitter can score a point.

A lot of practice is required to hit the ball accurately. This player is working on her bump pass.

Teams work together to set up passes.

The Spike

The spike! It is one of the most dramatic and dynamic single movements in all of sports. The sheer beauty and athleticism of a well-executed spike can take one's breath away. It is the home run, the slam dunk, the touchdown, the slap-shot goal, and the 300-yard drive of volleyball.

—Brad Saindon, head volleyball coach, Arizona State University

Watching someone spike is very exciting. It is a powerful smash over the net. The hitter slams the ball over the net and down on the opponent's side of the court. To spike the ball, the player must jump very high in the air, using perfect timing, and hit the ball powerfully, placing it so it is extremely difficult to return. The opposite of the spike is the tip. This is a lightly hit ball deflected or dropped into the opponent's court and is used by the spiker to surprise opposing blockers when they anticipate a spike.

Team defense is as important as it is to set the ball up to either win a point or get the ball back to your side. It is vital that the players prevent the spiker from the opposing team from getting the ball on their side of the court. At all times, the defense must be alert, anticipating and watching. They have to move along the net to the spot where they think the ball will be hit. The player opposite the spiker then has to jump up very high with fingers spread wide and block the ball. If the block is successful, the ball will fall back on the opponent's side, never reaching its anticipated goal. There are times the ball gets past the blocker, though. The rest of the team has to be on guard to handle the ball when this happens and defend their side. The members of the team get down very low to the ground by bending their legs. They stay low, close to the ground so they can dive for the ball. Sometimes the defensive player gets down so low to the ground that his or her body is stretched parallel to the floor. This movement is called a dig. Digs and other successful defensive moves are the most difficult shots and are therefore called saves. If the defensive play is good, it can actually save the game and contribute in a major way toward winning.

A good defensive team will be able to wear down and frustrate the opponent, forcing attack errors. Generally, the better defensive team will win close matches.

—Jim Stone, head volleyball coach, Ohio State University

The spike is probably the most exciting thing to watch in a volleyball match. This player has jumped high enough to spike the ball over the net.

Beach volleyball is typically played with two players on each team.
Here, you can see a beach volleyball game in progress in Gdynia, Poland.

Beach Volleyball

The rules followed for beach volleyball are slightly different from those followed for indoor volleyball. Beach volleyball is played by two teams of two members each. Instead of player rotation, the players alternate serves. The ball used for the outdoor game happens to be a little larger than the one for the indoor game as well as a little less inflated. The net is also elevated to 8 feet. One of the features of beach volleyball is the use of hand signals by players to indicate to their partner what sort of play they intend to make. The players signal to each other behind their backs.

Drills are like recipes. With the right ingredients and directions, anyone can cook, but it takes a master chef or a master coach to mix and vary ingredients to suit the needs of different individuals.

—Mary Wise, head women's volleyball coach, University of Florida

CHAPTER 3

Conditioning and Training

In most schools, volleyball is an essential part of the physical education curriculum. There are many practice drills that players can do in order to improve their game. Building up endurance, strength, timing, and coordination are important in the game of volleyball. Running can build endurance and stamina.

It is also important that players stretch so that they can dive for a ball. Stretching helps to become more flexible. Stretching is extremely important for players because the sport puts pressure and strain on body parts, especially below the waist. All that squatting, lunging, and digging can affect the body. Stretching raises your core body temperature and lubricates your joints, preventing injury. You can try this stretch: lie on your back with your head on the ground. Cross one

Stretching helps strengthen muscles that are important when playing sports such as volleyball.

ankle over the opposite bent knee. With your hands behind the bent knee, pull the leg into your middle until you feel a stretch in the back of the thigh. Make sure your head stays down in a relaxed position and increase the pressure only slightly each time you stretch. Repeat the exercise, reversing your legs and ankles. Remember, when you stretch it is important to hold for a count, and do not bounce.

It is necessary for players to be able to jump high in order to block. Jumping also helps in strengthening leg muscles. Drills such as jumping up and down as high as you can and jumping rope are good exercises. It is also essential in volleyball to have strong hands, especially fingers. Activities such as squeezing different sized rubber balls can assist in strengthening the hands. In order to make your hand more agile, you can alternately tighten your fist and then spread your fingers wide.

Players do all kinds of exercises to strengthen their thighs and arms, and to increase their stamina.

Practice Ideas, Dos and Don'ts

What you should do while serving:

- With underhand serves, stand facing the net with the foot opposite the hitting hand forward.

- Hold the ball at waist level.

- Lean forward and swing forward to contact the ball.

- Make sure that the hand holding the ball drops just before contact.

- Hit underneath the ball with the fist or heel of the hand.

- Follow through in the direction of the target with your hitting arm.

- With overhand serves, toss the ball 18 inches high, so the ball falls just inside the lead foot in line with your shoulder.

- Keep your elbow and hand at shoulder height or above.

- Shift weight to the lead foot, or step forward as you make contact with the ball.

- Make sure your wrist is firm throughout the serve.

- Contact the ball with the heel of the hand through the middle back of the ball.

- Make sure the contact sound is a thud, not a slap.

- Make sure your hand follows the ball to the target.

- Your serve should end with your hand alongside or within your body line.

When serving, it is important to keep your leg under your hitting arm behind your other leg.

Ivan Miljković is a Serbian volleyball player who is considered one of the best players in the world. He has won several awards. However, after 14 years and 288 matches, he retired from the national Serbian team in March 2012.

What you should not do while serving:

- Don't toss the ball so high that it is difficult to maintain control.
- Don't use the foot under your hitting arm.

Ideas for practice:

- See how many serves you can do in one minute.
- See how many good serves you can do in a row.
- See how many serves you can hit toward a specific target placed in the opposite court.

What you should do while passing:

- Start in the ready position.
- Use straight arms away from the body.
- Keep your knees bent.
- Contact the ball on your forearms.
- Face the direction you want the ball to go and aim the ball toward your target.
- Start out facing the server and always face the ball when you pass.
- Move toward the ball without crossing your feet.
- Try to anticipate where the ball will reach and get there first.

When passing, always ensure that your elbows are straight and your knees are bent. Here, you can see Emanuel Rego, a Brazilian player, in 2010 at Prague.

- Spread your fingers in the shape of the ball over your head when making an overhead pass.

- Form a triangle with your thumbs and pointer fingers; your hands should not touch each other.

- Place hands in front of the face close to forehead.

- On contact, set by extending arms and legs.

When making a pass, the volleyball should make contact with your forearms.

What you should not do while passing:

- Don't just stand there and do nothing.

- Don't bend your elbows.

- Don't swing your arms too much.

- Don't contact the ball unless your hands are together.

- Don't contact the ball with your upper arm or your wrist.

- In an overhand pass, don't contact ball with the palms of your hands.

- In an overhand pass, face away from where ball is coming from.

Ideas for practice:

- Three people—a hitter, a passer, and a digger—are all on the same side. The setter faces the passer and the hitter hits a down ball at the passer, who then digs it. The setter then sets the hitter. The drill is continuous and focuses on ball control with all three players.

What you should do while hitting, spiking, or blocking:

- Use approach steps and a two-foot jump.

- Use both arms for swinging forward on takeoff.

- Snap your wrist for topspin on contact.

- As you leave the floor to jump, pull your hitting arm back with the elbow and hand at shoulder height or higher.

- Have your hand open and relaxed with the palm facing away from the ear.

- Jump up vertically to meet the ball.

- Contact the ball at the peak of the jump with a straight arm.

- Land at least one foot past the contact point.

- Get the ball up the middle of the court so your partner can set it when it is a tough ball in beach volleyball.

- Play the ball low on defense.

- Spread your fingers wide, covering as much space as possible.

- Make sure your eye is always on the ball.

What you should not do while hitting, spiking or blocking:

- Don't jump on one foot.

- Don't hit the ball with a fist instead of an open hand.

- Don't swing one hand forward and the other behind.

- Don't use a shot-put arm action.

- Don't close your eyes when blocking.

- Don't close your fingers together when blocking.

Ideas for practice:

In pairs, one on each side of the net:

- Use the spike to hit across the net.

- Practice jumping before spiking.

- Practice spiking the ball against a wall.

These two players practice passing the ball to each other.

Nowadays, visualization is part of most sports training. Players imagine the play before executing it. For example, before serving the ball, the server visualizes where he or she wants it to land. This technique helps a player feel more centered and less anxious. Visualization also helps the player to think positively and enhances his or her ability to concentrate. Professional athletes and players even employ psychotherapists and coaches who specialize in training them to be proficient at visualization.

CHAPTER 4

Going for the Gold

In 1947, the Fédération Internationale de Volleyball (FIVB) was established, and the world championships were first played in 1949. Volleyball was added to the Olympic Games in 1964, and beach volleyball became an Olympic sport in 1996.

Russia *(in red)* and Algeria *(in green and white)* get ready to play against each other at the 2012 Olympics in London, U.K.

As soon as volleyball took off, it was very popular in schools and on the beaches, but it was still a relatively new sport to the Olympics. It was added as a medal sport in 1964 for both men and women. In the early Olympics, the dominating volleyball forces were teams from Japan and the Soviet Union (Russia). The Japanese women's team was coached by a man named Hirofumi Daimatsu. Their schedule for practice included training for six hours a day, seven days a week, fifty-one weeks a year. Daimatsu was a demanding coach, always wanting perfection, but he was often known to be verbally and psychologically abusive to his players. He taught the Japanese women a lot of new techniques, one of which was the rolling receive. This is when a player dives to the ground, smacks the ball, rolls over, and quickly stands up.

The Soviet Union became such a strong force that it was nearly impossible for any other team to beat them. The Soviet Union won the first men's Olympic gold medal for volleyball in 1964 and the fighting women's machine of Japan won the women's gold. In 1968, the Soviet Union again won the men's gold as well as the women's gold. In 1972, the Soviet Union's women's team won the gold, and in 1980, both the Soviet Union's men's and women's teams won the gold in Moscow. The Americans really wanted to compete against the Soviet Union, but the United States boycotted the Moscow games. President Jimmy Carter wanted to protest the former Soviet Union's invasion of Afghanistan and henceforth ordered all the American athletes to stay away from the Moscow Olympics. For the 1984 Olympics in Los Angeles, the Soviet Union decided to play tit for tat and boycotted the games. So in 1984, there was a change in the pattern of victories, and the U.S. men's volleyball team won the gold, and the U.S. women's team won the silver. The U.S. teams finally competed against the Soviet Union's teams in the 1988 Olympics held in Seoul, South Korea.

Team U.S. spikes the ball against Brazil in the final match for the Gold at the 2008 Olympics in Beijing.

Jon Root was a member of the American volleyball team that won the gold in the 1988 Summer Olympics.

Though the women's gold medal went to the Soviet Union's team, the men's gold was bagged by the U.S. team, which was led by players such as Karch Kiraly, Steve Timmons, Dave Saunders, Doug Partie, Jon Root, and Craig Buck.

There are many stars in volleyball. One of the most famous spikers in American volleyball history was a woman by the name of Flo Hyman. She was a member of the first group of U.S. women who trained together for the Olympics, beginning in 1974. She and her teammates also qualified for the 1980 Soviet Union Olympics, but because of the boycott they were unable to fulfill their dreams. In 1981, she was named the world's best hitter. "The audience would hold its breath when she rose for a spike," said Joan Ackerman-Blount of *Sports Illustrated.* Finally, in the 1984 Olympics in Los Angeles, Hyman and her team, challenged by the Chinese women's team, came in second to win the silver. Hyman, who was 6 feet, 5 inches tall, reported that winning the silver medal was one of the proudest moments of her life! By the end of the 1984 Olympics, Hyman was considered to be the best volleyball player in the world.

After the Olympics, Hyman played volleyball in Japan, where she was paid to play the sport she loved. In Japan in 1986, while playing a game, Flo Hyman collapsed and died. She was thirty-one years old. She lost her life to a disease called the Marfan Syndrome, which caused her aorta to rupture.

Karch Kiraly is the only player to have won Olympic medals in both indoor and outdoor volleyball. Kiraly is shown here at the AVP pro beach volleyball tournament at the Manhattan beach in 2006.

In honor of Hyman's achievement and work in support of women's sports, every year a young female athlete receives an award from the Women's Sport Foundation. In 1988, she was inducted into the Volleyball Hall of Fame in Holyoke, Massachusetts.

The Volleyball Hall of Fame was established in Holyoke, Massachusetts, in 1978.

Another great volleyball star, who retired in 2007, is Karch Kiraly. He is the only volleyball player in Olympic history to win three gold medals. He joined the national team in 1981 and led the U.S. men's volleyball team to two gold medals. He was also named the Most Valuable Player in the 1988 Olympics. Kiraly has an amazing jump serve. He tosses the ball with one hand while his other hand is on his hip. Kiraly established himself as an Olympic gold medalist in indoor volleyball and went on to play beach volleyball, where he won his third gold medal in the 1996 Olympics. Karch Kiraly has said, "Any beach is more attractive than the inside of a stadium . . . you have natural sunlight, girls in bikinis, guys in shorts. What better way to make a living than going to the beach?" Kiraly leads all pro beach volleyball players in career prize money.

Some other exciting U.S. stars in beach volleyball are Karolyn Kirby, Holly McPeak, Christopher "Sinjin" Smith, and Kent Steffes. Karolyn Kirby has won more event titles than any other woman on the pro beach circuits. Holly McPeak leads all women in career prize money with more than $1,000,000 in earnings. Christopher

Holly McPeak, three-time Olympian, shown here playing at the AVP Crocs Cup championship in Chicago in 2009, has won more prize money in her career than any other woman.

Smith is the oldest elite player in the world. He has competed in more beach volleyball events than any other player. Kent Steffes won the gold medal with Karch Kiraly at the 1996 Atlanta Olympic Games.

In 2016, the Olympics will be held in Rio de Janeiro, Brazil. The indoor volleyball competition will be held in the Maracanãzinho Gymnasium, which has a seating capacity of 11,800. The competition will last for more than two weeks, and the men's and women's matches will be held every other day. More than 280 athletes from different countries will participate in the Olympic volleyball championship. Beach Volleyball will be held at the Copacabana beach.

One can see how much volleyball has evolved when it is compared to the game that William G. Morgan had invented to keep men in shape. It is literally played around the world, and even beach volleyball is now considered as prestigious and serious as any other Olympic sport.

Wheelchair volleyball participants enjoy a game during a recent
United States Olympic Committee Paralympic Military Sports Camp at
the Naval Medical Center in San Diego, California.

Today, even the disabled can play competitive volleyball. The U.S. Congress passed the Olympic and Amateur Sports Act to give equal status to disabled athletes in 1988. The United States Olympic Committee (USOC) now organizes volleyball competitions for athletes in wheelchairs and those with other disabilities.

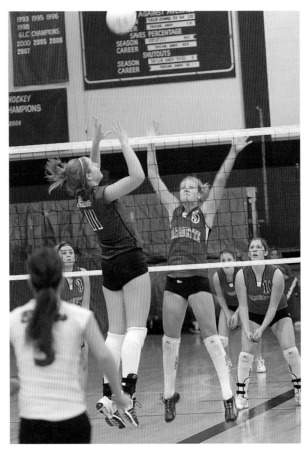

Most high schools and colleges have volleyball teams for men and women, such as this game between the Marquette Senior High School Redettes and the Gladstone Braves in Marquette, Michigan.

Players who are eighteen years of age, or younger, can compete in the Junior Olympic volleyball and Junior Olympic beach volleyball tournaments. But U.S. national volleyball competitions are open to players from thirty years of age to seventy-five years of age and older. There are volleyball leagues for players in grade school, junior high, and high school. No matter where you live, you can usually find a league for all age groups located close by. In order to locate the nearest reputable leagues, you may need to look in the telephone directory, browse the Internet, contact your local YMCA or recreation center, or ask your school physical education department.

Volleyball is being played around the world, and competitions for beach and indoor volleyball exist for players in various skills divisions and age groups.

Just as in any other sport, learning the skills and moves to play volleyball involves time, effort, and commitment. All it takes to become a good volleyball player is persistence, perseverance, and patience. Who knows, one day you might even become an Olympic star!

Olympic Indoor Volleyball Results for Gold

Year	Location	Women	Men
1964	Tokyo, Japan	Japan	USSR
1968	Mexico City, Mexico	USSR	USSR
1972	Munich, Germany	USSR	Japan
1976	Montreal, Cananda	Japan	Poland
1980	Moscow, Russia	USSR	USSR
1984	Los Angeles, California	China	USA
1988	Seoul, Korea	USSR	USA
1992	Barcelona, Spain	Cuba	Brazil
1996	Atlanta, Georgia	Cuba	Netherlands
2000	Sydney, Australia	Cuba	Yugoslavia
2004	Athens, Greece	China	Brazil
2008	Beijing, China	Brazil	USA
2012	London, United Kingdom	Brazil	Russia

Glossary

ace   A serve that scores a point without an opposing player touching the ball.

attack line   A line about 10 feet from and parallel to the net.

block   When a player jumping in the air uses his or her hands to prevent the ball from passing over the net.

bump pass   A volleyball pass made using one's forearms.

court   The area in which a volleyball game is played.

demarcate   To set the boundaries or limits of something.

dig   A move whereby a player hits a ball from below the waist.

endline   The lines along the breadth of the court that demarcates the court from the outside.

fault   An illegal move or play.

floater   A serve that is intended to float in the air before falling down.

forearm pass   A hit with straight forearms in front of the body, also called a bump pass.

game point   The point that will win the game.

inning   Each division of the game where each team has a chance of serving.

jump serve   A serve in which the server tosses the ball and then jumps to hit it.

kill   A shot that is impossible for an opponent to return.

match   Predetermined number of games.

net ball   A ball that touches the net.

overhand serve   A serve in which the server tosses the ball and hits it when it is above the head, but does not jump to hit it.

pass   To hit the ball to a player on your side with an overhead or a forearm pass.

rally The time when the ball is in play after being served.

rally scoring The kind of scoring used today, where either team has the opportunity to score a point.

reputable Having a good reputation.

rotation When a team gets the ball back to serve, players move one position clockwise.

save To keep the ball from hitting the floor, usually with a dig or dive.

serve To put the ball in play by hitting it directly over the net and into the other team's court.

set A high pass from one player to another.

sideline The lines along the length of the court that demarcates the court from the outside.

side out scoring The type of scoring used in the original version of the game, where only the serving team could score a point.

spike A rapid hit, usually after the ball has been set by another player, that sends the ball hard to the ground.

top spin A serve which is hit in such a way that it spins over the net.

underhand serve A serve in which the server tosses the ball and hits it by swinging his or her arm from below the waist.

visualization The act of forming a mental image of an action, event, or scene.

volley A series of plays in which the ball is hit back and forth between the two teams.

For More Information

Organizations:
American Volleyball Association
2134 East 2700 South
Salt Lake City, UT 84109
(801) 503-0888
e-mail: infovolleyball4all@gmail.com
Web site: www.volleyball4all.org

Disabled Sports USA
451 Hungerford Drive
Suite 100
Rockville, MD 20850
(301) 217-0960
e-mail: info@dsusa.org
Web site: http://dsusa.org

USA Volleyball
4065 Sinton Road
Suite 200
Colorado Springs, CO 80907
(719) 228-6800
e-mail: postmaster@usav.org
Web site: http://usavolleyball.org

USA Volleyball Beach Headquarters
200 Pier Avenue
Suite 134
Hermosa Beach, CA 90254
(310) 975-3930
e-mail: postmaster@usav.org
Web site: http://www.teamusa.org/USA-Volleyball

Volleyball Hall of Fame
444 Dwight Street
Holyoke, MA 01040
(413) 536-0926
Web site: http://www.volleyhall.org/

Magazines:

Volleyball Magazine
Madavor Media LLC
85 Quincy Ave., Suite 2
Quincy, MA 02169
(617) 706-9110
e-mail: info@madavor.com
Web site: http://www.volleyballmag.com/

Volleyball USA Magazine
4065 Sinton Rd.
Ste 200
Colorado Springs, CO 80907
(719) 228-6800
Web site: http://www.teamusa.org/USA-Volleyball/Mag

Web Sites

Due to the changing nature of Internet links, the Rosen Publishing Group, Inc., has developed an online list of Web sites related to the subject of this book. This site is updated regularly. Please use this link to access the list:

http://www.rosenlinks.com/STTS/Volley

For Further Reading

American Volleyball Coach's Association. *The Volleyball Drill Book*. Champaign, IL: Human Kinetics, 2012.

Bowman, John L. *The Art of Volleyball Hitting*. Bloomington, IN: AuthorHouse, 2013.

Couvillon, Artie. *Karch Kiraly: A Tribute To Excellence*. New York, NY: Information Guides, 2008.

Dearing, Joel B. *The Untold Story of William G. Morgan, Inventor of Volleyball*. Livermore, CA: WingSpan Press, 2007.

Dunphy, Marv and Rod Wilde. *Volleyball Essentials*. Oslo, Norway: Total Health Publications, 2013.

Hebert, Mike. *Thinking Volleyball*. Champaign, IL: Human Kinetics, 2013.

Martin, Peggy. *101 Volleyball Drills*. Montery, CA: Coaches Choice, 2010.

May-Treanor, Misty. *Misty: Digging Deep in Volleyball and Life*. New York, NY: Scribner, 2010.

Reynoud, Cecile. *101 Winning Volleyball Drills*. Montery, CA: Coaches Choice, 2007.

USA Volleyball. *Volleyball Systems & Strategies*. Champaign, IL: Human Kinetics, 2009.

Waite, Pete. *Aggressive Volleyball*. Champaigne, IL: Human Kinetics, 2009.

Bibliography

American Sports Education Program. *Coaching Youth Volleyball*. Champaign, IL: Human Kinetics, 2001.

Couvillon, Arthur R. *Sands of Time: The History of Beach Volleyball*. Hermosa Beach, CA: Information Guides, 2002.

Emma, Thomas. *Peak Performance for Volleyball*. Monterey, CA: Coaches Choice, 2003.

Gozansky, Sue. *Volleyball Coach's Survival Guide*. Paramus, NJ: Parker Publishers, 2001.

Scates, Allen E. *Complete Conditioning for Volleyball*. Champaign, IL: Human Kinetic

Shondell, Don. *The Volleyball Coaching Bible*. Champaign, IL: Human Kenetics, 2002.

Index

About the Authors

Sandra Giddens and Owen Giddens are the authors of *Chinese Mythology, A Timeline of the War of 1812, Everything You Need to Know About Crohn's Disease and Ulcerative Colitis, Coping With Grieving and Loss*, and *Future Techniques in Surgery.* Abigael McIntyre is a writer living in Montana.

Photo Credits

The photographs in this book are used by permission and through the courtesy of: Cover photo by muzsy/shutterstock.com; muzsy/shutterstock.com, 1, 16, 17; © Picsfive/shutterstock.com, 3, 15; © Markus at de.wikipedia/commons.wikimedia. org, 4; © Halter Leo, U.S. Fish and Wildlife Service/commons.wikimedia.org, 5; © Library of Congress/commons.wikimedia.org, 6; © The U.S. Army/commons. wikimedia.org, 7; © PikiWiki – Israel free image collection project/commons. wikimedia.org, 8; © Picsfive/shutterstock.com, 8, 39 © Own work/commons. wikimedia.org, 9, 13, 20, 21, 32; © Coppola Lino/commons.wikimedia.org, 9; © Christopher Halloran/shutterstock.com, 10; © almonfoto/shutterstock.com, 11; © d100/shutterstock.com, 11; © simonhorlick/commons.wikimedia.org, 12; © navy. mil/commons.wikimedia.org, 14; © Author Skipshearer/commons.wikimedia. org, 15; © Pal2iyawit/shutterstock.com, 16; © druchoy/Andrew Choy/commons. wikimedia.org, 17; © photofriday/shutterstock.com, 19; © Pukhov Konstantin/ shutterstock.com, 22; © holbox/shutterstock.com, 23; © Lucky Business/ shutterstock.com, 23; © dotshock/shutterstock.com, 24; © Gaspa/ commons. wikimedia.org, 25; © AndreyYurlov/shutterstock.com, 26; © Jamie Roach/ shutterstock.com, 27; © auremar/shutterstock.com, 29; © simonhorlick/commons. wikimedia.org, 30; © Craig Maccubbin/commons.wikimedia.org, 31; © zippy/ shutterstock.com, 33; © John Phelan/commons.wikimedia.org, 34; © zippy/ shutterstock.com, 35; © U.S. Navy photo by Mass Communication Specialist 2nd Class Greg Mitchell/commons.wikimedia.org, 36, 37; © Daryl Jarvinen from Marquette, Michigan, U.S.A/commons.wikimedia.org, 38.